The
Reformation
A Sound-bite History

The
Reformation
A Sound-bite History

Compiled by Andrew Cook

CHRISTIAN
FOCUS

Andrew Cook oversees production of Serving Today, the Grace Baptist Mission radio programme for pastors and church leaders. He has been with the GBM radio team since 2004.

Copyright © 2017 Andrew Cook
10 9 8 7 6 5 4 3 2 1

paperback ISBN 978-1-78191-986-6
epub ISBN 978-1-52710-019-0
mobi ISBN 978-1-52710-020-6

Published in 2017
by
Christian Focus Publications,
Geanies House, Fearn, Tain, Ross-shire,
IV20 1TW, Scotland, U.K.

www.christianfocus.com

Cover design by Daniel van Straaten

Printed by Nørhaven, Denmark

Front cover image is a drawing of the Heidelberg skyline.

Contents

Preface

Serving Today, a radio programme aired mainly in Africa, helps and supports pastors and church leaders in their ministry. Over the years *Serving Today* has been broadcasting short biographies outlining the lives, ministry and legacy of significant individuals from the history of the church. Many of these are well known, some others less so. While some have been influential among people of public office and power, all have served God and his people. Many suffered trials in the course of their lives and ministry, as do those that

Serving Today seeks to help. They come from different eras and historical contexts perhaps, but the calling to divine service is similar to ours today.

Once a particular series or topic comes to an end, a follow up booklet is produced on a small scale for listeners who request them. With the 500th anniversary of the Reformation in mind, it was suggested that something be produced to mark this important and significant date in 2017.

This short book is a compilation of some original audio biographies contributed to and aired on *Serving Today*. It is neither a definitive nor a comprehensive history of the Reformation, more in the nature of sound-bites of key events and characters who, under God, brought about a significant change in the life of the church. Some names are conspicuously absent, while the inclusion of others may be a surprise. So, for example, while George Whitefield lived over 200 years after the Reformation, his ministry and theology owes much, if not everything, to the Reformers who had gone before.

We are grateful to all those who have contributed to and continue to be part of *Serving Today*, each one a faithful and dedicated servant of Christ. We would particularly like to thank Philip Parsons who wrote (and recorded) most of the chapters that follow; Trevor Low for the material on Wycliffe and Latimer; and Philip Grist for the piece on John Calvin. The assistance of Don Crisp, Daryl and Julia Jones and my wife Marea also needs to be acknowledged for their help with editing and checking the manuscript.

We should also give thanks to those who ensured that the truth of salvation by grace, through faith alone as revealed in the Scriptures, continues to be proclaimed, to the glory of God alone.

Andrew Cook
Producer *Serving Today*
June 2016

Introduction

Why Study Church History?

As you will see as you read on, to read about church history is to read about our history, as the people of God, his chosen and loved church.

All history, particularly church history, is God's activity
We think of history as being what men have done, and so it is, but it is also primarily what God has done. The Bible teaches that Christ is the sovereign Lord of all history, the only one who has the right to open the seals of the scroll of history and reveal God's purpose in it

(Revelation 5). For other references which emphasise God's sovereignty over history see Daniel 4:34, 35; Ephesians 1:9-11; John 5:17; Revelation 17:17.

Above all, the Bible shows how this Sovereign God is working out His will and purpose in all history, which is truly HIS story.

The Bible is full of church history

Approximately half of Scripture is devoted to the record of God's dealings with His people. In the Old Testament, from Genesis to Esther, parts of Job, some Psalms and sections in the prophetical books are an historical record. In the New Testament, Matthew to Acts is predominantly historical, with other related references scattered throughout the epistles.

Perhaps someone might raise the objection that the history recorded in the Bible is part of the inspired Word of God and is in a different category to subsequent church history. That is true, but God is still at work within His church. Some of Hebrews 11 almost certainly refers to the inter-testamental period. We need to read post-biblical church history with discernment, but there is still much value to be had in studying it as God's work.

People in the Bible knew their church history

Several of the Psalms are what can be appropriately called 'Church History Psalms'. Some examples of this are Psalms 77, 78, 105, 106. Stephen's sermon in Acts 7 reviews a large portion of the history of the people of God during the Old Testament. If we followed the example of biblical writers and characters, we would be acquainted at least with the elements of the history of the people of God in all ages.

The people we study in church history are our brothers and sisters in Christ

They are part of the family of God to which we belong. They have gone to heaven ahead of us, but we are united to them by a bond stronger than flesh or blood. One of the glories of heaven will be meeting with God's saints from ages past. If you and I are going to get to know them in eternity then it seems strange that we should be wilfully ignorant of them while here below.

The Church has been the dwelling place of God throughout the centuries

We are related to the saints of old by the abiding presence of God in His church by His Spirit. This is illustrated by the promises of Hebrews 13:5 'Never will I leave you, never will I forsake you' and Matthew 28:20 'Surely I am with you always, to the very end of the age.' These promises are to all true believers in every age. It is a great comfort to know that we share this common bond with the people of God in past times.

What does church history teach us?

It teaches us that God deals with His people in sovereign grace

In a way, sovereign grace is the great theme of church history. God frequently chooses to work mightily at times which humanly speaking would seem to be the most unlikely. Often when the situation seems to be most antagonistic to any improvement, then God will act, partly to show that the work is His alone. For example in Luke 3:1-3, the political scene described by Luke could hardly have been less promising, yet it was at that very time that God chose to send John the Baptist to call the nation of Israel to repentance.

God will also often work through the most unlikely people. The apostles were mainly uneducated fishermen. Christ Himself was born in a seemingly unpromising human context. John Wesley and others among the eighteenth century leaders were initially unconverted ministers relying on their own works and 'holiness', yet it was through these men that God chose to turn the spiritual tide in England at a time when the gospel was largely unknown in the country, and even rejected by the established church.

History shows us that God often grants special blessing to His church through times of revival

This also follows the biblical sequence of events. Declension and revival are reflected in the whole of the Old Testament record. They have also been true of the work of God in subsequent history after Bible times. For example, even today we have not wholly lost the effects of the eighteenth century awakening. It was a group of Baptist ministers in Northampton who took up Jonathan Edwards' call to special prayer which led to the beginnings of the modern missionary movement. In a revival, more can be accomplished by one sermon than by many years of preaching prior to it. One of our problems today within the church in the West is that the majority are not convinced of the need for revival. If, however, Christians knew more church history, surely they would be convinced that revival is our greatest need? The biblical writers show their belief in this principle in the 'revival' Psalms (see Psalms 44, 74, 77, 79, 80, 85, 126) and also Acts 3:19, which speaks of 'times of refreshing coming from the Lord'.

Even apparent setbacks are part of God's long-term plan

Tertullian, one of the early Christians, said that 'the blood of the martyrs was the seed of the church.' When the English reformers were burnt at the stake in England in the 1550s, many who had followed them no doubt felt that all was lost. Cranmer, Latimer, Ridley, Hooper, Bradford and others all died under Queen Mary's persecution. And yet within a short while there had arisen a new group of men whose biblical teaching and living surpassed even that of the Reformers, the Puritans. In 1662, when two thousand

Puritan pastors were ousted from their churches and livings, it must then have seemed like a deathblow to the true church of God. Yet without the imprisonment of these men we would not have had so many of their writings, which have been a blessing to the church ever since.

A similar situation arose just before the Second World War. In Eastern Europe, there had been significant evangelistic advances in the pre-war years. Then came the war, after which the whole of Eastern Europe was annexed to the Soviet Union. Many young churches and new believers were then under a harsh persecuting regime, but in the sovereignty of God these Christians became the core of a sifted and purified church which in some countries saw significant revivals.

The thirty years of the Maoist era in China in the late twentieth century was another period of severe persecution for the church, yet in those thirty years the church grew more than in the previous 150 years of missionary activity. Hudson Taylor, the founder of the China Inland Mission in late Victorian England, would be amazed at the growth of the church in modern-day China.

We can observe the errors of past times and seek to avoid them

Most modern errors and false teaching have appeared in some form or another in previous times. The Jehovah's Witness teaching denying the deity of Christ had its counterpart in the Arian heresy of the fourth century. The excesses of the modern Charismatic movement are similar to early nineteenth century Irvingism and second century Montanism. Widespread ignorance of church history is one reason why the church often falls into errors which it has fallen into before. Church history, rightly understood, can act as a corrective to tendencies towards erroneous and unbiblical thinking.

God has preserved His church even through the darkest times

Among many interpretations of the two witnesses of Revelation 11 we would hold that the best one is that it refers to those times when the true church of God seems to have almost expired. Yet even in such dark times, like the Middle Ages, there were true believers and God raised His church to life again. John Calvin speaks of the many resurrections of the church, of which the Reformation was probably the greatest ever seen.

So, why might we neglect church history?

WE HAVE BEEN AFFECTED BY THE SPIRIT OF THE AGE

We live in a generation dominated by an evolutionary mindset which, as a result, tends to regard the past in a dismissive and patronising manner. This philosophy argues that there has been so much progress over the last hundred years or so that anything previous to that has been regarded as primitive. However in recent years there are some signs of a change in this pattern of things. There have been some very good history programmes in the media, some of which have shown that the ancients were not quite as primitive and ignorant as 'modern man' might have supposed. However the idea that 'the old is of little value' still persists, even among some Christian groups.

The way history was taught at school and biblical history in Sunday School

At school history was often taught as a sequence of dates and political developments with no spiritual perspective. Even in Sunday School Bible stories tended to be taught in isolation from how they fitted into the framework of biblical history. Think back to how you were taught about the Reformation at school – if you were! It was a largely political event, with Henry VIII breaking from the Church of Rome because he wanted to divorce his first wife. This, however, is only a very small part of the story and ignores the great spiritual movement which was taking place all over Europe at that time.

The 'New Testament and us only' position

This point of view looks at church history through sectarian spectacles and regards many past eras of the church (the New Testament excepted) as being so much in error that they are not worth considering. This was certainly true of the Brethren background from which I came. I don't remember hearing anything at all about the Reformation or the Puritans or the eighteenth century evangelicals. A modern example of this sectarian mentality towards church history is found in the twentieth century Charismatic movement. Some Charismatics can find little in church history which corresponds with their brand of theology other than their claim to be at one with the early church. So in general Charismatics have no interest in the study of church history, or only very selectively. You may sometimes hear the phrase 'the early and latter rain'.

The importance of what we are seeking to cover in this booklet was summed up by Martyn Lloyd-Jones: 'I know of nothing more instructive, next to the Bible, than church history' (*Authentic Christianity*, Vol. 1, p 147). The Psalmist says, 'Walk about Zion, go round her, count her towers, consider well her ramparts, view her citadels, that you may tell of them to the next generation.' (Psalm 48: 12-14)

Chapter 1

The Reformation, its Origin, Principles and Effects

Five hundred years ago, on 31 October 1517, an apparently insignificant event occurred which has had a profound effect on subsequent European and world history. A German Augustinian monk, Martin Luther, nailed a document to the door of the castle-church in Wittenberg in Saxony (central Germany). Luther's action sparked off a powerful movement, which has become known as the Protestant Reformation, often referred to simply as the Reformation. In the opinion of one twentieth century evangelical theologian,

Professor John Murray, 'the Reformation (was) … the greatest revival of faith since the days of the apostles'. Although not all would agree with this view of the Reformation, the translators of the Authorized Version of the English Bible did. In the preface to that Bible they refer to it as 'our blessed Reformation'.

In this chapter we briefly look at three aspects of the Reformation: its origin, principles and effects.

ITS ORIGIN

No great movements in history occur in a vacuum, and the Reformation was no exception. Just think of the conditions prevailing at the time. The whole of life in Europe was dominated by the largely corrupt medieval church. You couldn't be born without the aid of the church through infant baptism, you weren't allowed to live without observing the dogmas and practices of the church and you couldn't even be buried without the permission of the church. Even kings and princes had to take account of the church's power which, through its priests and the whole hierarchy up to the Pope, controlled all of life. For such an apparently invincible system to be shaken to its very core, as it was by the Reformers, surely marks out the Reformation as one of God's greatest works in history. Some of the circumstances which gave rise to the Reformation and which clearly demonstrate its divine origin are outlined below.

It was a movement from within a largely corrupt church. 'Largely corrupt' because, despite the almost total control of life by the medieval church, there were groups of Christians who had managed to remain free from many of the false teachings of those times. One of these groups was called the Waldensians, who lived in a remote mountainous region of northern Italy. But God did not use the Waldensians to bring about the change. They were themselves affected and renewed, but the work started elsewhere, within the mainstream medieval church. In one sense, the spiritual darkness which prevailed immediately before Luther produced his protest document was seen for what it was, once the light began to shine again from the pages of Scripture. Even so, only divine power could have produced such a fruitful work from such barren ground.

Moreover, the movement that we now call the Reformation simultaneously sprang up in many different places at once. Once Luther had nailed his Theses document to the church door at Wittenberg, it was as though this was just what people had been waiting for. Within two months the '95 Theses' had been circulated, translated and printed throughout the whole of Europe. Even the Pope had been given a copy! It had not, in fact, been Luther's aim to start a popular movement of such magnitude. He had intended that theologians and scholars debate the theological points. Yet it was as though there was a tinder-dry forest just waiting to be set alight and Luther's document was the match. Subsequent to his simple and unremarkable act on that fateful

31 October 1517, he said himself that it was as though he was being pushed and jostled and carried along by a power totally outside his control. It wasn't because of his personality or some powerful human organisation – it was God at work.

It was a movement that was aided by the comparatively recent invention of the printing press. Pamphlets, books, Bibles etc. could all now be produced in quantity in a very short time. Previously they had been copied laboriously by hand. God's perfect timing was thus evident even in the use of the then relatively modern technology of printing.

The way had also been prepared by another remarkable event. In the fifteenth century the Turkish Empire was expanding and in 1453 Constantinople (modern Istanbul) fell to their armies. It was the fall of this great city to the Turks that resulted in many of the writings from the early centuries of the church now being scattered across Europe. Up to that time, the monks in Constantinople had jealously guarded these writings, which included copies of the New Testament in Greek. As the Turkish army advanced upon the city it was feared that when the city was taken, many of these Christian books would be destroyed, so they were smuggled out of the city before it finally fell. The spread of this literature across Europe was certainly one factor in the birth of the pre-Reformation movement called the Renaissance, 'Re-birth' (of knowledge), which in turn helped to pave the way for the Reformation.

DOMINANT THEOLOGICAL PRINCIPLES

It is profitable to study the lives of the Reformers as individuals. When we do, we find our spirits stirred and our faith strengthened. It is equally important to know why they did what they did, because they were mere humans just like us, and yet they turned their medieval world upside down.

The principles which underpinned the Reformation have been described by the following five Latin phrases: *Sola scriptura* (Scripture alone), *Sola gratia* (grace alone), *Sola fide* (faith alone), *Solus Christus* (Christ alone) and *Soli Deo gloria* (to the glory of God alone).

Scripture alone

It was not easy for those steeped in the medieval church's teachings to reject the notion of an infallible church and embrace instead the authority of the infallible Scriptures to which the fallible church must submit. But God gave the Reformers grace to do so and as a result we have the legacy of this first and foundational Reformation principle, as important today as it was then. The Reformers believed that all questions of doctrine and life must be settled by Scripture. It is true that they were not always able to work through the principle in every area of church life. Sometimes this was because of restrictions placed upon them from a hostile State. In some instances it was because they themselves could not let go of some of the traditions to which they had held all their lives. But Martin Luther could say, 'My conscience is captive to the Word of God.'

This is not just of academic interest, for the truth of the Bible is constantly being challenged today, sometimes in quite subtle ways. It may begin with the undermining of an unpopular teaching according to the prevailing culture of the age, such as creation or eternal punishment, but that will inevitably lead to an outright denial of the heart of Christian truth, the Gospel itself. Or it may be that some man-made tradition is put alongside the Bible and given equal weight with it. Under the pressure of human thinking, the tradition will become more important and dominant. A high view of Scripture has been a real help to some when wrestling with evolutionary ideas. Accepting the truth and validity of the book of Genesis in the face of Darwin's supposed scientific views has led to the strengthening of their faith.

Grace alone

This principle raises the vital question: do men and women in any way assist in their coming to Christ? In other words, have they free will to choose to be saved? The answer from the Bible is that it is all of sovereign grace. Luther saw this very clearly as a conflict of free will versus free grace. The first major public debate of the Reformation, which took place in Leipzig in 1519, was on the subject of the will, which from Scripture Luther saw as bound, not morally free. We too need to be reminded of this today. One of the biggest hurdles to evangelism is the emphasis on free will. Those whose 'evangelism' involves asking people to make their own physical response to the Gospel are betraying the fact that they do not really trust the Holy Spirit to do His work; they feel they have to give Him a helping hand. But God will not share this work with us, however sincere we may be. As a result, modern 'decisionist' practises in evangelism have been largely a failure and have produced large numbers of false converts as the passage of time shows. It is not modern techniques or modern methods but the true Gospel of the free grace of God preached in the power of the Holy Spirit which will change hearts and minds.

Faith alone

In Luther's experience it was the words of Romans 1:17, 'The righteous will live by faith', which first shone light into his soul. As a devout Augustinian monk he had believed that he could only ensure his salvation by his own performance of good works and observance of church dogma. 'If ever monk could have been saved by his monkish works then I would have been,' he said. Yet by God's grace, resulting from his study of Paul's letter to the Romans in the New Testament, he began to see that all had been done by another (Christ) and that all the benefits of His saving work were to be received by faith and faith alone. 'That night,' he said, speaking of his conversion, 'I fell into the arms of a loving heavenly Father.' Of such importance did Luther consider this principle to be, that in his translation of Romans 3:28 into German he used the word 'alone' for emphasis although it is not in the original Greek text.

It is perhaps this principle above all others which marks out biblical Christianity not only from all other religions but from all deviant forms of the Christian faith. On the surface they will speak of the importance of faith for salvation, but when you probe them you will find that they believe our 'good deeds' contribute in some way to our salvation. The question for us is, do we stand where Luther did? We begin the Christian life by faith alone and it must be by faith alone that we continue to stand, so that when we come to depart this life our comfort will not be drawn from what our hands have done, but only from the finished work of Christ on our behalf.

Christ alone

This follows on logically from 'faith alone' because if we do not have the right object of faith it is a useless faith. Many have some kind of faith today, but how many really do trust in Christ alone and in His finished work? There are so many things that can draw us away from the simplicity of the Gospel of Christ. In medieval times it was the belief that grace came through the works of the saints. Modern Catholicism still in effect places Mary, the mother of Christ, as an object of faith above her Son. The danger for some is to have a misplaced faith even in the sheer orthodoxy of what they believe, but if they do not go from the teaching they receive about the person of Christ to the person Himself, then they are little better off than those who do not believe such teaching. The question is, have we really entrusted ourselves to Christ alone in the face of all the issues of life and death? If we have Christ we have everything, without Christ we have nothing.

The glory of God alone

Luther's great question as a young man was, 'How can I be saved?' In later years he turned to a deeper question: 'How can I glorify God?' Surely, it is this question and how we answer it that will have a profound effect not only on what we do, but also the way we do it. So much of what is done for God can often be done with mixed motives and a large measure of self-gratification. How important it is that what is done for God is because of a desire to bring honour and glory to Him. It is even sadly possible to be so busy in God's work that we forget the paramount need to seek His glory. May *Soli Deo gloria* once again become a principle among Christian believers.

If we can really grasp these five Reformation principles and hold tenaciously to them, we will not go far wrong. Inasmuch as any church departs from these, it is drifting away from its Reformation roots. May God grant His church further reformations and renewings, of which the church is always in need.

Most major events in history have had repercussions which affect life in this world long after the event itself. The Reformation is no exception, having long term effects both on church life and wider human society.

Effects of the Reformation on church life

A return to the simplicity of New Testament church order

Before the Reformation there was a vast hierarchy of church clergy, including the whole array of cardinals, bishops, priests, monks, nuns, friars etc., with the Pope at its head. All these offices had grown up over the centuries but we find no support for them in the New Testament. There is also very little evidence of them in the history of the early centuries of the church. The Reformers saw clearly that the majority of these so-called spiritual offices were of human origin. On much of the Continent and in Scotland, where there was less interference from the state, the standing offices in the church were reduced to elders and deacons. In England the situation was complicated by Henry VIII making himself the head of the Church. In some ways it seems incredible that after five hundred years, the Church of England still has the monarch as its head. With regard to church reform, any abolition of the monarchy would completely change the position and power of the bishops as well.

There is another relevant point to consider. It may not have escaped your notice that nowadays the media always refers to all ministers in the church as priests. However, the Bible teaches that with the coming of Christ, the office of priest has completely changed. Christ is our great High Priest and there is now no divinely ordered office of priest among men, as there was in Old Testament times. There remains only the 'priesthood of all believers' by which all believers offer spiritual sacrifices to God and plead with Him in prayer for their fellow human beings.

The recovery of the simplicity of true Christian worship
The form of worship we have in most Nonconformist churches today is very similar to that of the Reformed churches on the Continent and in Scotland in the sixteenth century. Even the design of buildings is significant, where the pulpit is usually central and dominant, emphasising the importance of preaching God's Word. This finds its biblical basis in Nehemiah 8:4-5 as well as in New Testament teaching and practice. In contrast to the plainness and simplicity of post-Reformation church buildings, one of the first things which strikes you when you enter a non-Reformed church is that the altar is central and dominant. In Reformed churches everything is simple and plain. There is no longer an altar. There are no elaborate rituals or special clothes. There are no images or pictures of the saints. This is no accident or minor issue, rather it is central to Reformation theology. It was the simplicity of the eastern European Reformed Churches which surprised the Islamic armies when

they spread westwards towards Vienna in the sixteenth century.

We owe the simplicity of our worship to the Reformation. Sadly, other things are creeping back into the worship of God even in evangelical churches. In some places candles have been reintroduced supposedly to symbolise prayers. Paintings and tapestries depicting the person of Christ are reappearing. The simplicity of worship in truly Protestant churches is a great gift from God which we should cherish and maintain.

The recovery of biblical expository preaching

In the days of Christ and the early church, it was preaching which turned the world upside down (Matthew 3:1, 2; 4:17). In times of Christian revivals, it has always been preaching which has come once more to the fore, whereas in times of spiritual decline, preaching becomes marginalised. Before the time of the Reformation the same principle applied. There was some preaching in the medieval church, but it was often wholly allegorical or a kind of moralistic rant. Truly biblical preaching was almost unknown, with the exception of John Wycliffe in fourteenth century England and John Huss and Jerome in fifteenth century Prague. In our day, some evangelical churches have begun to drift away from their Reformation moorings back to things akin to medieval practices. We should be aware that the introduction of more music and drama may risk marginalising the preaching. In the Reformed churches, the sacraments were always secondary to the preached Word whereas the opposite was true in pre-Reformation times. If we denigrate and marginalize preaching then it will not be long before we lose it and the sacraments begin to dominate again. Preachers are a great gift to the church. If we despise the gift, then God could well withdraw it from us.

The importance of the prayer meeting

Did you know that the prayer meeting as we know it is a fruit of the Reformation? Within the orbit of the medieval church, the concept of corporate extempore prayer was virtually unknown. There may have been some exceptions, but the rule was that it was the priests and the monks (the professionals) who did the praying. This shows the low level of true living faith in those times, for where there is true faith then there is a desire to pray together. So the prayer meeting has become part of our Protestant heritage. We must guard it zealously and hold on to it. It has been rightly said that the state of the prayer meeting in any church is a measure of the spiritual health of that church.

The proper division between church and state

The proper roles of church and state and their relationship to each other can be summed up in the words of Jesus, 'Give to Caesar what is Caesar's, and to God what is God's.' (Luke 20:25). In many countries today the state interferes with the affairs of the church. The problem in medieval times was rather that the church was dominant and interfered with the state. Rulers felt that they had to get permission from the Pope for their actions, although in England after the Norman Conquest and Magna Carta, there was an increasing independence from Rome. Following the Reformation, the distinct roles of church and state began to be redefined. This process took some time, different countries moved forward at different rates. In England the full development of the Reformation was curtailed by the premature death of Edward VI. As a result, the Church of England has never become completely disentangled from the state. This principle is really one of authority. If the rightful authority of Scripture were re-established, then neither church nor state would dominate, each would have its own distinct and proper sphere.

WIDER EFFECTS OF THE REFORMATION

Many of the values upon which our western society has been based historically, and has grown and flourished, find their source in the Reformation. The reality of this truth means that those who try to disparage or discredit the Reformation are in effect undermining the foundations of our western society, although they often don't realise it. There are exceptions. In the TV series 'Seven Ages of Britain', the presenter Bettany Hughes, clearly saw the Reformation as foundational to our modern society.

Let us consider some of the by-products of the Reformation which mark out our culture both from medieval society and from cultures based upon other religions.

The right of private judgement

This principle means that individuals have the right to think for themselves, to make up their own minds and express their own opinions. This privilege springs from the right of everyone to read and study the Scriptures for themselves. This might seem to us an obvious privilege, but is not so obvious if you live under a dictatorial regime dominated by Communism, Catholicism, Eastern Orthodoxy or Islam. Before the Reformation, anyone who did not agree with the dictates of the Church had to keep quiet about how they thought, or else they could be tried for heresy. Merely possessing a fragment of Scripture in English in the fourteenth century was a capital offence. Even following the Reformation, this freedom did not change overnight. It took many years before true religious freedom became enshrined in the laws of western European nations and it is a myth to think that such freedom would ever have occurred apart from the Reformation. The more that our society today reverses the principles for which the Reformers laid down their lives, the more we will find our freedoms eroded.

Literacy and education

Obviously there was some education before the Reformation, but literacy was encouraged and stimulated by the availability of the Bible in mother tongues throughout Europe, and by the right for all to read it for themselves. It was famously William Tyndale's aim that the ploughboy should be able to both read and understand the Scriptures. Henry VIII's son Edward VI, probably the godliest king that England has ever known, established grammar schools, some of which are still functioning today. The Sunday School movement, set up in the early nineteenth century, was originally an attempt to give education to the poor. The first Sunday Schools were nothing like those of today, but taught poor children to read and write. They were held on Sunday because it was the only day that Christians could give for this, away from their daily work.

The Protestant work ethic

In the Middle Ages there was a supposed spiritual hierarchy of work, the work of the clergy being considered as more spiritual than others. We have already seen that most of this 'spiritual' hierarchy was not Biblical. Other 'lay' occupations were considered to be non-spiritual and of a lesser order.

The Reformation brought back the concept of the sanctity of all work, with no one sphere of activity being considered *per se* more spiritual than others. This is in fact what the Bible teaches, that all lawful occupations are honourable in and of themselves. For the Christian, all work should be worship because we are following the example of our Creator, Sustainer and Saviour. After all, Jesus spent the greater part of His life employed in manual work as a carpenter. The Bible teaches us to, 'Do it all for the glory of God' (1 Corinthians 10:31) and, 'Whatever your hand finds to do, do it with all your might' (Ecclesiastes 9:10). Again, it says, 'He who has been stealing must steal no longer, but must work, doing something useful with his own hands' (Ephesians 4:28).

Because work is God-given, it should be seen as more than just an opportunity to earn money and to live as a Christian in an unbelieving world. It means that in all our work we should aim to be the very best that we can be. In fact, it could be argued that the quality of our work is a more important part of our witness than anything we *say* about our faith in the workplace. Sometimes Christians can be unwise and actually do damage to the cause of Christ by spending their employer's time in trying to proselytise, then turning in rather shoddy work. We should seek to shine in our callings, which in itself will have a much greater impact than many words and will support our words when we have a legitimate opportunity. By all means let us speak to our work colleagues about our faith, but in our own and not our employer's time!

The result of the Protestant work ethic is seen in the material progress which has been achieved by the Protestant nations in western culture. One of the great values of Christians in the workforce is that such things as honesty, integrity and conscientiousness are displayed in the lives of these Christians, which in turn have a real impact upon a company's prosperity and a nation's economy. The problem we have today is that these principles have been seriously eroded and this is undermining the very fabric of our society. Just think of the huge amount of money which has to be raised in taxes to cover 'new' policies and practices which actually break the Ten Commandments. Consider the dishonesty that goes on at all levels. Think of all the money that is spent because of the wholesale disregard for marriage (seventh commandment), or in providing extra housing as a result of family break-up, or treating sexually transmitted diseases such as HIV/AIDS. In western society we are squandering the wealth which previous generations have gained for us.

Selfless concern and enterprise

It is no coincidence that many of the founding fathers of modern science and technology were Christians and had the influence of godly principles on their lives. One modern writer claims that out of more than fifty leaders of the post-Reformation scientific revolution, more than 90 per cent were professing Christians. Think too of all the great social reformers such as William Wilberforce, Lord Shaftsbury, Elizabeth Fry and Dr Thomas Barnardo, who were Christians. It would be wrong to say that there could be no progress in science or the caring professions without a strong evangelical influence, but it cannot be reasonably denied that a great impetus was given in these areas by the efforts of dedicated Evangelicals, who put the glory of God and the welfare of their fellow human beings above the desire for personal gain or recognition.

CONCLUSION

We have a great heritage in both church and national life which is being attacked today, in some cases quite blatantly. The wholesale undermining of the Christian principles which have been the basis of the greatness of western progress is alarming, and if allowed to continue could well plunge us back into a kind of medieval night dominated by false religion of all kinds including militant atheism and secularism. If the moral and spiritual decline continues, then surely we are in for dark days ahead. Yet all things are in the hands of a Sovereign God.

Let us pray that God will act in mighty power to turn the tide, but also, for our part, let us aim to be faithful to the principles of the Reformation in every area of our lives and to do all within our power to resist and protest against the appalling decline, whether in our churches or in the nation at large.

Chapter 2

Martin Luther

Of all the individuals involved in the Reformation, Martin Luther stands out as a key driving force, whom God greatly used.

His early life

Coming from peasant stock, the son of a miner, Martin Luther was born into humble surroundings in Eisleben in Germany on 10 November 1483. He was called Martin because the following day was Saint Martin's Day, one of the many saints honoured by the

Roman Catholic Church. As a young child he was sometimes carried to school on his father's shoulders. Because he was a bright lad, at the age of fifteen he continued his schooling away from home in Eisenach where he had relatives. It seems that these relations were unable to provide for him sufficiently, for he and some of his friends sometimes used to sing from door to door, hoping to receive money towards their food. One good lady, Frau Ursula Cotta, took pity on Luther and invited him to eat with her on a regular basis. There he began to mix with more educated company than he had previously known. At the age of eighteen he went on to the University of Erfurt, where he began to distinguish himself in his studies. It was then that he first came across the Latin Vulgate, the Latin translation of the Bible. As he read it, he was deeply impressed, particularly with the story of Samuel's call as told in 1 Samuel chapter 3.

After completing his university course at the age of twenty-two, several events occurred which would completely change his life. Firstly, one of his student friends was killed in a brawl and Luther immediately thought, 'What if that had been me?' There followed further close brushes with death. On one occasion he accidentally cut into an artery and another time he was caught out in a violent thunderstorm. As he lay on the ground in fear he cried out for help to Saint Anne and vowed that if his life were spared he would become a monk and serve God in a monastery. He did survive the thunder and lightning so he duly fulfilled his vow and entered the monastery of the Augustinian order of monks in Erfurt, much to the annoyance of his father who had hoped for a more lucrative career for his son.

LUTHER'S CONVERSION

By this time a deep desire for peace with God had taken hold of him and he hoped that the monastic life would give this to him. But if he thought that the religious life would make him acceptable to God, he was soon to be disappointed. Behind monasticism lay the idea that if only we could escape from the evil world around us, then we could live holy lives that are pleasing to God. The fatal flaw with that view is that it takes no account of the evil within our own hearts. Luther certainly found this to be so in the monastery. Because he seemed to make no real headway against his sins, he tried all the harder in his religious exercises, with long periods of fasting and beating himself. This zealous young monk soon caught the eye of the vicar-general of the Augustinian order in Germany, a man named von Staupitz. He was a wise and spiritual man and used his position to act as a kind of travelling pastor to the monks. He gave Luther much good advice: he encouraged him to eat better and not to fast so often, to get more sleep and above all, to study the Word of God. Von Staupitz later recommended Luther for a teaching position in theology in the newly established university in Wittenberg. Luther still lived in the monastery but lectured in the university each day.

As Luther began to study the Scriptures, it was the early chapters of the book of Romans which shone light into his soul, particularly Romans 1:17, 'The righteous will live by faith.' When he understood the real meaning of these words he said that it was as though the gates of paradise had been opened to him. We can justifiably consider that this was the point of his conversion which he described as 'falling into the arms of a loving heavenly father.' He clearly came under great conviction of sin and this lasted for many months, if not years. Some of the greatest men of God have had similar experiences of deep conviction of their sin such as John Bunyan and George Whitefield.

Luther's visit to Rome

Because of his connection with the monastery, Luther was sent on a special mission to Rome in 1510 to represent the German Augustinians there. He was delighted with this opportunity for, to a zealous medieval Catholic, Rome was as Mecca is now to a modern Muslim. Again he was in for another shock. As the historian James A. Wylie describes it, 'Instead of a city of prayers and alms, of contrite hearts and holy lives, Rome was full of mocking hypocrisy, defiant scepticism, jeering impiety and shameless revelry.' (James A. Wylie, *History of Protestantism*, Vol. 1, p. 254)

It was, in fact, while in Rome that he took another step away from the doctrines of the Catholic Church. To the devout Catholic there were many pious acts which could be performed to gain merit both for oneself and for others. One such act was to ascend the so called *Scala Sancta* (Sacred Stairway) on one's knees, saying the Lord's Prayer on each step. It was as he was doing this that the words, 'The righteous will live by faith' came again into his mind, almost as if a voice spoke them to him. When he came to the top of the stairway the thought also came to him, 'What if, after all, my actions achieve nothing?'

As we consider Luther's spiritual state, we might perhaps think that at his conversion he should have seen that the supposed good works which the church prescribed were worthless. But the fact of the matter is that old habits and ideas die hard. This is consistent with the New Testament letters, mostly written to young Christians, some of whom had come from a completely pagan background. Paul has to exhort them to stop lying and stealing as clearly some had continued in this way of life after conversion. When Luther came to an initial (if limited) understanding of the doctrine of justification by faith alone, he was still a loyal member of the Catholic Church and still held to many of its erroneous views and ideas.

Yet Luther's visit to Rome was an experience which had further opened his eyes to the false doctrine and corrupt practices of the Church. In later life he valued it as a worthwhile experience, particularly when he was tempted to doubt the rightness of reform, and when he realised that the work of Reformation meant a complete break with the Church of Rome.

THE 95 THESES

Returning to Wittenberg, Luther soon received the degree of Doctor of Divinity and in 1515, aged thirty-two, he began to preach in the parish church. The people heard his biblical expositions gladly and many flocked to listen to his sermons. But events were to occur which would thrust the young Luther into the spotlight and make him a household name right across Europe.

The Pope had decided that he wanted to rebuild Saint Peter's Basilica in Rome. This required a huge amount of money, which was to be raised mainly by the sale of Indulgences. For the payment of a suitable sum of money, it was taught that a certain number of years could be taken off one's time in purgatory. According to Roman Catholic teaching, purgatory is a kind of halfway-house between this life and heaven. You could also buy an Indulgence for a dead relative. This was one way by which the church in those days had a spiritual hold over the hearts and minds of the faithful. One particular man selling these Indulgences throughout Germany was a monk from Leipzig, called Tetzel. He was very good at extorting money by pulling at the heartstrings of the recently bereaved. He was so bold that this rhyme was used to sum up the essence of his message, 'When the coin in the coffer rings, the soul from purgatory springs!' When Tetzel came close to the town of Wittenberg, however, not everyone approved of this seller of Indulgences, whose life was also a known scandal. Frederick, Duke of Saxony, refused permission for him to enter the region. Tetzel came as near as he could to the border, about an hour's walk from Wittenberg, and crowds flocked from the town to hear him and buy his Indulgences. Luther was appalled and sprang into action. At first he began to warn his congregation in his sermons, but his opposition to these Indulgences soon came to the ears of Tetzel himself. Tetzel poured out a torrent of abuse against the man who would dare to oppose his mission, since it was approved and endorsed by the Pope.

As well as a preacher, Luther was by now professor of Theology at the University of Wittenberg. How would he respond to Tetzel's teaching about Indulgences? Luther was always a man of action. His plan was this; he would spell out in some detail his objections to Tetzel and his sales of Indulgences, and would do this by using the accepted method of the time. He wrote out his objections and pinned them to the church door where other public notices were displayed. He chose to do this to coincide with the very popular festival of All Saints which fell on 1 November. So on 31 October 1517, the eve of All Saints Day, Luther made his way through the crowds and nailed what are now referred to as the '95 Theses' to the church door. Immediately people began to read the document and great interest was aroused. It was soon copied, printed and distributed all over Germany, and within four weeks it had been translated into the other major European languages. Even the Pope had a copy!

It is interesting to note that the theses were in fact quite mild in their tone. They were clearly against the doctrine of Indulgences but were very deferential towards the Pope. They were still far from the theological position which Luther eventually came to, yet this was the document which sparked off the Reformation. At this point in time, however, no one could have anticipated the far reaching impact this document would have. No doubt Luther himself had no idea of the great significance of his actions. In truth, the events of 31 October 1517 were part of God's sovereign dealings with His church to bring it back to its biblical and apostolic roots. The Reformation was under way, there could now be no turning back. Luther has been rightly described as 'The monk who shook the world.'

ROME'S RESPONSE

At first the Pope did nothing, perhaps hoping that it would all quickly die down. However, the '95 Theses' had produced such a stir across the whole of Europe that they and their author could not be ignored. Several attempts were then made to persuade Luther to change his mind. At first, threats were made by one of the Pope's representatives, Cardinal Cajetan.

Then pressure was applied to Frederick, Duke of Saxony, who was sympathetic to Luther's position. A public debate was also held in Leipzig which only strengthened the case that Luther was making. One of the main topics discussed was the human will; do we have free will to choose to follow Christ or are our wills hopelessly enslaved to sin? In emphasising the bondage of the will, Luther showed a clear break with medieval scholastic thinking. Finally on 15 June 1520 the Pope issued a 'Papal bull', a document condemning Luther and ordering that his writings be burned. In response, Luther burned a copy of the bull in public to show his contempt for its contents.

We can see at this point that Luther had moved on from the position he held at the publication of the '95 Theses', where he had been very deferential to the Pope. By now, he had come to realise that the Pope and all that he stood for were an essential part of the Church's departure from the truth of God's Word.

CHARLES V AND THE HOLY ROMAN EMPIRE

We need to step back at this point and take into account an important stage of European political history going back 700 years before this event. At that time, the Pope was pleased with the way that Charles, King of the Franks, had helped him to subdue the unruly citizens of Rome. As a reward, Charles was invited to Rome to be crowned officially by the Pope. This act by the Pope in A.D. 800 created what was later to be known as the Holy Roman Empire with Charles as its first emperor.

In 1520 a new emperor was chosen, Charles V, King of Spain, and Frederik, Duke of Saxony was one of those involved in his appointment. One of the things that the emperor did was to hold a kind of court, called a Diet. He would have held it in Nuremberg, but due to political unrest in Bavaria it was decided that it should be in Worms. Wishing to show himself to be a loyal son of the church, Charles summoned Luther to the Diet. Because of the threats against his life, Luther was advised not to go. He was, however, a man of great courage and conviction and determined to attend, set out from Wittenberg in early April 1521, arriving in Worms on the sixteenth of that month. By this time, Luther had become a kind of international phenomenon and the crowds that gathered in the streets when he entered Worms were as numerous as those who would gather to greet a conqueror returning from victory. It has to be added that many in the crowds were hostile to Luther, a monk who was brave enough to stand up and oppose both church and Pope. In fact, the next day when he and his supporters attempted to go from their lodgings to the Diet, the streets were so thronged that it was only with great difficulty that they managed to reach the conference hall where the Diet was to take place.

LUTHER BEFORE THE DIET AT WORMS

The Diet was by any standards a brilliant and imposing assembly. There was the emperor, his six electors and many other high-ranking men of church and state, including dukes, margraves, archbishops, bishops, abbots, ambassadors and deputies of free cities. In all there were 206 people representing most of Europe and the whole church. On a table, all Luther's writings were displayed and he was asked two questions: were they his writings, and would he retract those doctrines in them which were contrary to the teachings of the church? Luther examined the books and acknowledged that he was their author. He requested more time to consider the second question and the proceedings were adjourned until the following day. Luther spent much of the night in prayer and by the providence of God, we have an extent copy of that prayer recorded.

> O God, my God, be with me and protect me against the enemies of the world. Thou must do it, Thou alone, for in me is no strength. It is thy cause, O God, not mine. On thee I rely, not on man, for that would be in vain. O God, dost thou not hear? Do not hide thy face from me. Thou hast called me, now be my stay. I ask it in the Name of thy Son, Jesus Christ, my protector, my shield and my defence. (S.M. Houghton, *Sketches from Church History*, p. 89)

The next day, 18 April 1521, was perhaps the most important day in Luther's life, described by one writer as, 'One of the sublimest scenes which earth has ever witnessed'. The question was put to him again as to whether or not he would withdraw his writings. His reply, first made in Latin and then repeated in

German, lasted for about two hours. It ended with these immortal words,

> Unless I am convinced by testimonies of the Scriptures or by clear arguments that I am in error – for popes and councils have often erred and contradicted themselves – I cannot withdraw, for I am subject to the Scriptures I have quoted; my conscience is captive to the Word of God. It is unsafe to do anything against one's conscience. Here I stand; I cannot do otherwise. So help me God. (S.M. Houghton, *Sketches from Church History*, p. 89)

The Diet was infuriated by this response. Having been granted a safe-conduct by the emperor, Luther was allowed to leave Worms unharmed on 25 April. A few days later, however, the Diet agreed that he should be placed under the ban of the empire, so that any who harboured or sheltered him would be liable to a charge of high treason against the emperor.

CAPTURE AND IMPRISONMENT

Though Luther did not yet fully realise it, he was in serious danger. After a few days of travelling, he and his companions entered the forest of Thuringia. Suddenly they were surrounded by a group of masked horsemen who seized Luther and carried him off into the forest. Under cover of darkness he was taken to a nearby castle, where he was told that he must disguise himself as a knight and take a new name and then remain hidden until it was safe for him to leave. Where was he?

The next morning as he looked out of the window he realised that he was in the Wartburg castle which overlooked the town of his upbringing, Eisnach. Frederick, Duke of Saxony had organised Luther's capture and secret imprisonment as a kind of protective custody, but to the world at large, he had vanished into thin air.

How was he to spend his time? Like the other reformers, he realised that his desire to bring people back to the Word of God was hampered because the common people had no access to the Scriptures in their own language. He set about translating the New Testament into German, with the first draft being completed in just eleven weeks! By 1522 it was on sale in Germany for the equivalent of a craftsman's week's wage; even at that price there was great demand for it, and copies sold rapidly.

It is also significant to note that while Luther was in Wartburg castle, events outside were working for the spread of the Reformation. The Turkish emperor Solyman was advancing into Eastern Europe. Meanwhile, war broke out between France and Spain, forcing the emperor Charles V to return home. The Pope, Leo X, seemingly in good health, suddenly became ill and died so quickly that there was no time for him to be given the last rites. The new Pope, Adrian VI, although no friend of the Reformation, was so different from Leo that those around him found it difficult to adjust to his attempts at reform. All these factors meant that for a while the spotlight was taken off Luther and the reform movement at Wittenberg.

LUTHER RETURNS TO WITTENBERG

Yet problems now arose, even at this centre of the Reformation. There were some who were much more radical in their views than Luther and they wanted not only to dispense with the Pope and all the errors of the medieval church, but they wanted to throw out the Bible as well. Like many of those who depart from or reject God's Word in our own day, they claimed to have a higher authority than the 'Word of God'. These 'Zwickau prophets', as they were called, were threatening the whole cause of the Reformation.

As soon as Luther heard about these recent developments in Wittenberg, he decided to leave the security of his hilltop fortress to seek to stabilise matters. On his return, he spent a whole week in discourse emphasising the need for caution on matters of reform and emphasising the supreme authority of the Scriptures, which the German people would shortly have in their own language. The radicals were banished by the power of the Word and the course of biblical reformation was once again maintained at Wittenberg.

AN INCOMPLETE REFORMATION

Yet it seems that these events which threatened the course of the Reformation did in fact influence

Luther himself. Another factor was the peasants' war, a movement which began in the south of Germany. As it gained momentum it threatened to engulf much of Central Europe. Thomas Munzer, one of the extremists who emerged in Luther's absence from Wittenberg, took a leading role. At first Luther attempted mediation, but neither the authorities nor the peasants took any notice of him. When all-out war broke out, he sided with the Princes. One hundred thousand were killed in the resulting conflict, but it hardly touched Saxony where the Reformation had had its profoundest effect. The actions of Luther in breaking with the Church of Rome had, however, clearly added impetus to this civil unrest. This must have hurt him deeply and perhaps accounts for why he was unable to develop his reforms further.

After 1522 he made little further progress on the path of reformation, but retained some doctrines and practices which we might have expected him to have rejected as unbiblical.

The Lord's Supper

The sacrifice of the mass, one of the cornerstones of catholic theology, had been rejected as such at Wittenberg, but Luther was unable to discard some remnants of it in his celebration of the Lord's Supper. He held to a view called 'consubstantiation', that although the bread and wine did not actually change into the body and blood of Christ as church dogma taught, in some mysterious way the body and blood of the Saviour 'were present alongside the elements'. His entrenchment in this position was totally opposed by Zwingli, one of the early Swiss reformers, who saw the Lord's Supper as only a memorial meal. Calvin and other later reformers held a view somewhere between Luther and Zwingli, that the communion was to be received as a means of grace to the faithful and humble participant. Unfortunately, Luther's view of the sacrament caused a rift with the Swiss Reformed Churches, although they were able to draw up the Marburg Confession covering those points on which they were agreed.

Veneration of images

In the early days of the Reformation, there arose groups of extremists who would travel from place to place pulling down all religious images, both those outside and those inside buildings. Some of these acts caused considerable damage to buildings and property and Luther, appalled at the trail of wreckage, reacted in an opposite direction and allowed images such as crucifixes to be kept in churches.

Despite these reservations we must not underestimate the key role which, under God, Luther played in the Reformation. Others were able to move on from where he left off, perhaps the most important of them being John Calvin. Luther had, as it were, set the forest ablaze and as such his work was done. It is often true that God allows great men to have feet of clay so that we will be less tempted to give them the glory which belongs to God alone.

LUTHER'S LAST DAYS

There is much that has been omitted from this brief life of the great reformer: about his wife and children, his home life, his wise and witty comments at mealtimes (now encapsulated in the book *Luther's Table Talk*), his eloquence in the pulpit, and so on. But space does not allow expansion of these themes.

We cannot however conclude our study without reference to his death. Ever since the edict of the Diet of Worms putting Luther under the ban of the empire, Luther's life had been in danger from his enemies, yet none were able to touch him. In early 1546 he was away from home near to the place of his upbringing, Eisleben, when he was taken ill, probably with some kind of heart condition. On 17 February, realising that his end was near he offered a final prayer and died peacefully in his bed.

It cannot be over-exaggerated how keenly his loss was felt. To those around him, it was as though the sun had set. They transported his body back to Wittenberg and as it came nearer to the town, the crowds following and those lining the road swelled in such number that it resembled an army on the march. He was buried in the castle church at Wittenberg, the very place where his '95 Theses' had been nailed to the door.

Briefly to summarise the main characteristics of Luther's life:

He was a truly spiritual man, a man of prayer, who walked closely with his God.

He was a man of great courage, who when he saw the way of truth, followed it unflinchingly.

He loved and preached the Word of God. The study of the Scriptures had brought him into spiritual liberty so he taught and preached that word to others. His phrase, 'My conscience is captive to the Word of God' will remain with us for ever.

He and his companions gave the German people the Scriptures in their own tongue. The publication of Luther's German Bible was the first time that any people group had the Scriptures translated directly from the original Hebrew and Greek into their own language.

The influence of extremists was one reason why Luther pulled back from further reform. The way of extremism is never right; it is often a device of the devil to seek to undermine God's work and bring it into disrepute. God, however, is not dependent on any particular individual and others were raised up to continue his work.

As we thank God for the Reformation, so too we should thank God for Martin Luther, for he was the human instrument used by God to begin the work. As with any true man of God, 'Their deeds will follow them' (Revelation 14:13).

CHAPTER 3

John Wycliffe

Now we go back to fourteenth century England as we consider John Wycliffe, whose influence on Bible based Christianity was and remains revolutionary.

EARLY LIFE

John Wycliffe was born in the county of Yorkshire in northern England sometime between 1324 and 1330. At the age of about fifteen he went to Oxford University. In those days, students did not simply study for three or four years to get a degree, but for nine or ten years for a Bachelor of Arts, followed by a further eight or nine years specialising in theology. Eventually, he became a Professor in Divinity at Oxford University and was known as the 'Flower of Oxford'. As Oxford was already one of the leading universities in Europe at that time, he was probably one of the most eminent scholars in Europe in the fourteenth century.

THE CHURCH IN ENGLAND AT THE TIME

The church had many offices, involving large numbers of people, including monks, nuns, friars, priests and bishops. Unfortunately, the church in the fourteenth century was largely corrupt, one of its false teachings being that sins could be forgiven by the paying of money to the church. There was very little true faith in the Lord Jesus Christ and very little regard for the teaching of the Bible.

WYCLIFFE'S CONVERSION

It was as a student that Wycliffe was truly converted to Christ. At the time, a terrible plague known as the Black Death was spreading throughout both England and the rest of Europe and it was reckoned that somewhere between a third and a half of the population died from this contagion. This created in Wycliffe a great fear of death and of judgement, causing him to cry to God for mercy. He then came to repent of his sin before God, and began to read the Bible for himself. Consequently, he soon realised that the teaching of the church was not the same as the teaching of the Bible, and that was when he really made it his life's ambition that the ordinary people of England should have the Word of God in their own language. Up to that time, much of what was taught in the church was in Latin which ordinary people did not understand. When Wycliffe asked himself why people did not realise that they were being taught error, he realised that the answer was because they were being taught in Latin and that they did not know any different, and could only accept what the church taught.

TRANSLATING THE BIBLE

John Wycliffe is most famous for translating the Bible from Latin into the common language of the people. This was in about 1380. Within little more than two years he had most of the Bible translated, helped almost certainly by other friends and colleagues. Wycliffe believed very firmly that the ordinary people should have the Bible in their own language, which is exactly what he sought to bring about.

This desire and purpose to translate the Bible into English proved to have a great cost to Wycliffe himself and to his followers. The church in those days did not want its practices to be seen as wrong or its authority challenged. It did not want the truth of the Bible to come out, perhaps above all because it was making so much money from the false ideas in its teaching. Wycliffe was brought before various church courts and threatened with being expelled from the church or worse, but he was faithful to what he believed was his calling from God. This included not only translating the Bible, but gathering a number of men around him to preach and spread the truth. They became known as Lollards. The name almost certainly came from a word meaning 'to babble', a rather derogatory term that people would apply to him and his followers just as some did of Paul in New Testament days (Acts 17:18). But those called Lollards were in fact lay preachers who went out into the countryside and preached the truth of the Word of God to ordinary people.

The Mass

In 1380, having first delivered lectures on the subject, Wycliffe wrote a piece entitled *On the Eucharist* which shook the church. In the eyes of ordinary people, the power of the clergy came in part from the priest's ability through his ordained office, to turn the bread and wine into the actual body and blood of Christ. This is called the doctrine of Transubstantiation. Wycliffe showed how this teaching was in fact comparatively recent, having only officially been accepted in 1215, and that it was entirely contrary to Scripture. He was in fact challenging the priestly power of sacrifice: a priest without a sacrifice, he argued, is no priest at all. If ordinary people are not dependent on a priest to work this 'miracle' on their behalf, then they are no longer in slavery to the priest and can come directly to the Saviour Himself.

To translate the Bible was one thing, to criticise the church was another, but above all to deny the sacrifice of the Mass was unthinkable to those accepting the authority of the church. For Wycliffe it marked the end of the support of many who had up to that point been sympathetic to him.

In 1381, an Oxford commission threatened anyone holding Wycliffe's opinions with suspension from the University and even being thrown out of the church. In response, Wycliffe published a defiant paper named 'Confession' in which he defended his viewpoint.

LEARNING FROM THE LIFE OF WYCLIFFE

One of the reasons for learning about important figures in the history of the church is to consider what lessons we can learn from their lives. Obviously, there is John Wycliffe's own personal faith in the Lord Jesus which he came to through his study of the Bible. Secondly, his belief that everyone has the right to hear the truth of the Bible, be that through reading it or having it preached to them. Thirdly, there is his sheer perseverance in the face of many difficulties and hardships: people hounded, tried and pursued him but he stuck faithfully to the work God had called him to do.

HIS DEATH AND LEGACY

Wycliffe died on the last day of 1384, in his mid to late fifties. We should be thankful to God for his life, because he established the principle of making the Bible available in the common language of the people, which was, of course, English in Wycliffe's case. However, the principle applies to all spoken languages around the world and it is appropriate that Wycliffe Bible translators, the organisation dedicated to making the Bible available to all people groups around the world, is named after the man himself.

Key to the Reformation was the truth that the Bible's own teaching was of more importance than the teaching of men, a principle held by Wycliffe many years before the movement became widespread. In this, he prepared the way for people like Luther and Calvin, and is rightly remembered as the 'Morning Star of the Reformation'.

CHAPTER 4

John Huss

There is no direct link between Wycliffe and Luther, but a man named John Huss provides an intermediate connection, so we now turn our attention to this champion of the faith in Europe.

EARLY CHRISTIANITY IN BOHEMIA

John Huss came from a central European country then called Bohemia, whose capital was Prague. Christianity did not come to Bohemia until about the eighth century, and even then many of the early converts were merely nominal. In the ninth century, however, the king of Moravia, a neighbouring country, requested that the Scriptures be translated into the local language.

With the Bible available in their own language, God blessed its use, so that a large number of people in Bohemia were converted. Over the next 200 years, Bohemians were able to worship and read the Scriptures in their own tongue. However, by the late eleventh century the Pope imposed the reintroduction of church services in Latin and banned the use of Bibles in the language of the people. Evangelical influences were not altogether lost, for around that time a number of Waldensian refugees came into the country, fleeing persecution in the mountains of northern Italy. These people were zealous evangelists, not in public gatherings but by teaching in private houses. As a result, they kept alive a purer faith than was taught and practised by the Roman church. Under the protection of some members of the local nobility, some churches continued to worship in their own language, which also helped to prevent Bohemia from falling into total spiritual darkness.

In the mid fourteenth century, King Charles of Bohemia was elected as the Emperor of what was then called the Holy Roman Empire. One of his achievements was to set up the University of Prague with the aim of making it equal in learning with Paris and Oxford. Charles was succeeded by his son, the famed King Wenceslaus, who forged a link with England by arranging the marriage of his sister Anne to King Richard II. Anne was a godly woman who loved the Word of God and encouraged the writings of John Wycliffe to be brought into Bohemia.

The stage was set for the appearance of God's man for the hour, John Huss.

THE PREACHER OF PRAGUE

Against this background John Huss was born in 1369. He grew up as a peasant in the village of Husinetz, from which he seems to have taken his name. John Huss' father died when he was quite young, and his mother was helped with the cost of his education by a rich nobleman who presumably recognised his potential. Huss did not disappoint his mother or their rich patron. By the age of thirty-four he had been appointed rector of the University of Prague, one of the highest possible academic attainments in his nation. Around this time, an event occurred which was to be a turning point in his life. Ten years earlier in Prague a chapel had been opened called the Bethlehem Chapel, dedicated to the preaching of God's Word in the local language. In 1402, Huss was appointed its preacher. He began to speak out against the many sins and vices of his day, so much so that he seemed to be a kind of conscience for the nation. As well as his direct study of Scripture, he also studied the writings of John Wycliffe. It appears that, by the grace of God, it was in the course of preparation and delivery of his sermons at this time that the preacher himself became spiritually awakened.

Another event also helped to open Huss' eyes. In the church in Wilsnack there was a supposed relic of the blood of Christ, said to possess miraculous powers. People flocked from all over Bohemia and beyond in the hope of obtaining a cure for various diseases. Many doubts were, however, raised about the genuineness of the miracles claimed to take place, so the Archbishop of Prague appointed a commission, including Huss, to investigate. Of the many cases which were examined, that of two women said to have been cured from blindness was questioned. It transpired that they had only had sore eyes and had never been blind. In 1405 the Archbishop prohibited pilgrimages to the blood of Wilsnack.

It was not long before Huss' preaching in Prague came to the attention of the Pope, particularly when Huss began to speak out against the sale of Indulgences. This led to the public burning in Prague of books by John Wycliffe which had been influential in bringing Huss to his convictions. Huss himself was then summoned to Rome. He was advised not to go, so the Pope condemned him in his absence and ordered that all the churches in Prague be closed. Altar lights were put out and images were covered over with sackcloth. Huss was forced to withdraw from Prague to his native town of Husinetz. Although unable to preach in Prague any longer, he spent much of his time travelling around the country, preaching in other towns and villages to great crowds. During this period, Huss came to a clearer understanding of the doctrine of the Church, and wrote a treatise expanding his newly-found views. This book entitled *On the Church* proved to be a great help to Luther, a hundred years later.

THE COUNCIL OF CONSTANCE

Clearly the Church of Rome could not tolerate this state of affairs for much longer, but a fundamental problem of their own prevented decisive and united action. At that time there were three rival claimants to be Pope, one in Italy, one in Spain and one in France. Before any effective move could be made against the movement for reform, this division had to be healed. The new emperor, Sigismund, also king of Bohemia, decided to call a church council and so in 1414 the Council of Constance was convened.

The Council was very splendid. It included the emperor, kings and other nobles from all over Europe, as well as cardinals, archbishops, bishops and priests, each with an entourage corresponding to their rank. It has been estimated that the city of Constance had an influx of around 100,000 people. The first business of the Council was to settle the question of the 'true' Pope. In the event, all three rival Popes were deposed and a new one elected.

John Huss the Heretic

The Council then turned its attention to the reformer, John Huss. Huss had only agreed to come to the Council on the basis of a 'safe-conduct' granted to him by the Emperor. However, despite this guarantee he had not been in the city for more than a few weeks before being arrested and thrown into prison. He was confined for six months in a damp, unhealthy dungeon situated on the banks of the river Rhine, next to where the main town sewer emptied into the river. At his first appearance before the Council, Huss was unable to speak in his own defence because he was shouted down by many of the clerics opposed to him. Soon it became clear that the Council had already determined to condemn him. Only a full recantation of all those beliefs which in any way conflicted with the tradition of the Church would save him. He refused to do this and eventually, in July 1415, he was sentenced to death by burning at the stake.

So ended the life of John Huss. When he was finally fastened to the stake, he is said to have uttered these memorable and prophetic words, 'It is thus that you silence the goose, but a hundred years hence there will arise a swan whose singing you will not be able to silence.'

The legacy of John Huss

Huss' ideas were in some ways less advanced than those of Wycliffe. For instance, he never came to a clear understanding of the doctrine of the Lord's Supper.

His view was probably similar to Luther's, whereas Wycliffe had come to see that transubstantiation was not a Scriptural teaching. On the other hand, Huss did begin a reform movement among the population of Bohemia which continued for a few decades after his death, and which for a while successfully challenged the power of the Roman church. As with Wycliffe and Luther, the touchstone was his understanding of the Scriptures. He asserted the right of every individual to read and hear the true teaching of the Bible and to find salvation in Christ alone.

Chapter 5

John Calvin

CALVIN'S EARLY YEARS

John Calvin is definitely among the greatest theologians of all time. No other theologian has influenced the Christian Church worldwide more than this great and gracious man.

He was born in 1509 in the north-east of France, where he was the son of a church lawyer. His father intended him for the Roman Catholic priesthood and so from 1523 to 1528, he studied at the university of Paris. However, when his father quarrelled with some clergy in the Roman Catholic Church, he decided that his son John should not become a priest. As for Calvin himself, he was at this time a Christian humanist, a philosophy that seeks to unite the Christian faith with classic humanist ideas.

Sometime in the 1530s Calvin, influenced by two friends, embraced Protestant teachings. He speaks of, 'A sudden conversion, God subdued my heart to a teachable spirit. Thus, having gained a taste of true godliness, I burned with great zeal to make progress.' However, trouble soon arose! In the face of growing opposition to Protestant truth Calvin escaped into hiding, by disguising himself as a gardener. At that time, a violent persecution broke out in Paris against Protestants and twenty-four were burned at the stake. In 1535, Calvin fled to Basel in Switzerland.

CALVIN'S GREATEST WORK

It was in 1536 that Calvin began writing his famous book *Institutes of the Christian Religion*. Soon this twenty-six year old scholar came to be regarded as the foremost champion of French Protestantism. The *Institutes* was an orderly summary of Christian doctrine and life. After he completed it in 1539 it became the standard textbook for reformed theology. Over the years, Calvin added to it and the final edition in 1559 became four books! Reformed gospel teaching can be summed up as, 'Salvation by God's grace alone through faith alone in Christ alone to the glory of God alone.' No other book has so influenced evangelical thinking right down to the present day.

BASEL, STRASBOURG AND GENEVA

Calvin stayed in Basel for over a year. He then moved to Strasbourg where he hoped to settle and live a quiet life. However, a visit to Geneva changed all that. There he met William Farel, a man likened to a fiery Old Testament prophet. Farel wanted Calvin to stay, but he first made excuses that did not impress Farel, who is said to have called down the curse of God on Calvin for wanting to live a peaceful life amongst his books. Through Farel's outburst, Calvin felt that God was calling him to stay. So, it was in Geneva that Calvin lived out almost all the rest of his life. He came to share Farel's desire and vision to see Geneva becoming a model Christian community. However, in April 1538 both Calvin and Farel were officially banished from the city over a dispute on the issue of the Lord's Supper. Farel settled near Berne and Calvin went back to Strasbourg where in 1540 he met and married a French lady, Idelette de Bure. They had one son who sadly died in infancy and then in 1549, his wife also died.

It was in Strasbourg that Calvin was to form a life-long friendship with Philip Melanchthon. Calvin spent three happy years in that city, where he was greatly used of God in bringing churches together. Whilst Calvin was a naturally gentle, quiet and rather shy person who detested controversy, in the service of Christ he was strong and powerful, utterly consecrated to the Saviour's will.

CALVIN UNDER ATTACK

A certain Roman Catholic cardinal was highly critical of Calvin and tried to win Geneva back to the Roman Catholic Church. In the face of this attempt to crush the Reformation there, many of the citizens of Geneva pleaded with Calvin to return. Of Geneva, Calvin said, 'There is no place under heaven that I am more afraid of.' Eventually, yielding to the urgent appeal, he went in fear and trembling saying, 'I offer my heart a slain victim in sacrifice to the Lord.' Even though so many of the citizens wanted him back, he knew it would not be an easy pathway. Indeed the future years saw many struggles. For instance, he longed for the Lord's Supper to take place in churches every Sunday, but in those days he had to apply for permission from the city magistrates, who would only licence it four times a year! Even so, Calvin's vision continued for Geneva to be a 'Christian city'. There were, however, many political opponents and there was bitter conflict between Calvin's supporters and opponents.

During his years in Geneva, Calvin wrote and published many important works including his 'Genevan Catechism', and many of his Bible commentaries plus a whole series of sermons. Indeed, the number of books he published is quite staggering, many of which are still available today, translated into many languages including English.

FINAL THOUGHTS

Calvin's achievements are often thought of as one of the most significant and successful aspects of the

Reformation of the sixteenth century. In addition to what has already been said, Calvin not only wrote but encouraged the translation of the Psalms into French by a poet of the time. These would be used in singing the praises of God. They were to be sung to simple but lively tunes, many based on popular melodies. He provided reformed churches with clear, solid theology. He also gave them a pattern of church government still used today. He showed the world a city (Geneva) that actually sought to live out the faith. Lastly, he made the reformed faith the great missionary movement of his day

Calvin was taken ill in the autumn of 1558. He feared he might die before completing all his additions to the *Institutes*. He did however recover. Later he seriously strained his voice preaching and brought on a fit of violent coughing which burst a blood vessel in his lungs. From then on, his health steadily declined. His final sermon was preached in February 1564 and he passed into his eternal rest in May of that year. His body was laid in an unmarked grave. Whilst there is today a grave in Geneva traditionally regarded as Calvin's, in fact the exact location of his burial remains unknown. So ended the life of one of the greatest theologians the world has ever known.

CHAPTER 6

Hugh Latimer

We next consider the English reformer, Hugh Latimer. We are all to a great extent the product of the times in which we live. In order to appreciate fully the man and his influence, his courage and his faith, we must look at the spiritual condition of England at the time of Latimer's life.

It was in 1517 that Martin Luther nailed his '95 Theses' to the door of the Castle church of Wittenberg in Germany, exposing the darkness of the established church. At that time England was under the rule of Henry VIII, while her religion was increasingly dominated by Cardinal Thomas Wolsey. For the majority of the population, spiritual darkness and superstition reigned. Most priests and church men were themselves ignorant of basic Bible knowledge. One writer records that many of them could scarcely say the Lord's Prayer or the Ten Commandments. Prayers were said in Latin which hardly anyone understood. There was little preaching and what there was, was unbiblical and unhelpful.

Around the country were many monasteries and abbeys but largely these were dens of inequity and immorality. It is well established that weak and dying people were persuaded to give their money to these monasteries and abbeys, under the guise of being taught that they would be accepted by God on account of these 'good works'. The church claimed to hold the keys to the Kingdom of Heaven, so confession of sin had to be made to a priest who alone could grant absolution and forgiveness. Without a priest, no one could be saved.

We can understand, therefore, why people who knew only such teaching were terrified of the power and displeasure of the church. If you so much as bought a Bible you were considered a heretic. The only concept of how to get to heaven was to do as the priest said; it was a case of the blind leading the blind. Prayers were made to the saints and to the Virgin Mary. There was a famous shrine in the city of Canterbury in England – a shrine to a former archbishop called Thomas Becket. It is reckoned that 100,000 pilgrims each year made their way to Becket's tomb in order, as they believed, to help their souls towards heaven. In one particular year, there was offered on Christ's altar three pounds, on the Virgin Mary's altar sixty-three pounds and on Thomas Becket's altar eight hundred and thirty-two pounds. This shows the order of the priorities the church taught and established. Images, relics and saints bones, most if not all them complete frauds, were all objects of worship. The church taught and enforced these things on the people, all of whom were their parishioners. This was the state of religion in the early sixteenth century in England and this was so-called Christianity during the childhood and youth of Hugh Latimer.

HIS EARLY LIFE

Latimer was born in 1485 in the county of Leicestershire in the middle of England. His father was a farmer. Hugh was educated in the local schools and gained a place at Cambridge University. He graduated with a masters degree in 1514. Having been raised in a staunchly church household, he was himself an ardent church man at university. Indeed, his zeal won him the right to carry the university cross through Cambridge in the annual parade. He did this for seven consecutive years, a great honour indeed. Meanwhile he would attend lectures given by George Stafford, one of the university lecturers. Stafford differed from the others in that he taught directly from the Bible. At the time, however, Latimer often attended Stafford's lectures with the sole aim of putting him off and causing disruption. In one sermon later in his life, Latimer said, 'Until I was over 30 years of age, I used to think that I could be saved by the law.'

When he became a Batchelor of Divinity, in 1524, he was expected to give a lecture to the university. He chose as his theme Philip Melanchthon and his teaching. Melanchthon was one of the great reformers in Germany and a close friend of Martin Luther. Still an ardent churchman, Latimer used his lecture to attack the German reformer's teaching and to defend the church's teaching. He also warned his hearers against meetings which were currently being held in the White Horse Inn in Cambridge. There a group of students would meet to read and study the Bible. They were led by a man called Thomas Bilney. Bilney was as enthusiastic about reading and teaching the Bible as Latimer was about ritual and the outward show of religion. While Latimer delivered his lecture, in the audience sat Bilney who decided there and then to try to win this fanatical church man to the Reformation cause.

HIS CONVERSION

Having given his lecture Hugh Latimer returned to his room, proud to be called the champion of the established church. Thomas Bilney followed him, knocked on his door and immediately took the initiative by saying, 'Be pleased to hear my confession.' Latimer invited him in, thinking that he had regained his erring brother by his lecture. However Bilney had not come for absolution but for confrontation. He told Latimer of the anguish of heart that he had once felt, of his own efforts to find peace with God and of how he had found forgiveness of sin only through trusting in Christ and his redeeming death. Latimer found himself confronted with the true Gospel; by the grace of God, he was convicted and converted. In a sermon years later, he said, 'I learned more through Bilney's confession than I had done in many years. From that time forward, I began to love the Word of God.'

He who had previously been the university's cross bearer, now took up the cross of Christ in biblical terms and became a sufferer for righteousness sake. Instead of preaching tradition and ritual, he preached the Gospel. Needless to say, he and Bilney became firm friends and he joined the group at the White Horse Inn in Cambridge, as they discussed theology.

But years of indoctrination take a long time to shake off and for some years Latimer remained unclear about some aspects of church teaching. For example, he continued to believe in transubstantiation, which is the belief, as taught by the church, that the bread and the wine literally turn into the body and blood of Christ.

HIS EARLY MINISTRY

Although he was not the greatest theologian of his day, he was certainly the best preacher. He preached to scholars at Cambridge in Latin, but with equal effect would preach to the ordinary people in English. He realised that England had been starved of the true Gospel and now found that his calling was to feed the masses with the bread of life. As a farmer's son, he could easily relate to the working people.

It goes without saying that Latimer's new stance brought opposition and enmity. The church sought to trap him and catch him preaching heresy. On one occasion, the Bishop of Ely entered a church while Latimer was preaching. Latimer stopped, waited for the bishop to be seated and then changed his theme and text. He spoke from the text, 'Christ came as high priest of the good things that are already here' (Hebrews 9:11). He preached on the spiritual responsibilities of priests and especially bishops. At the end the bishop came to him, thanked him for his sermon, though Latimer realised that that was all a sham, and then asked Latimer if he could help by writing an article denouncing this vile German reformer, Martin Luther. Latimer recognised the trap being laid for him and said, 'I'm afraid I would be unable to do that since to do it, I would need to read Luther's works, and the church forbids us to read those works.' He took his leave with the words, 'I'm sure I have preached before you today no man's teaching, but only the teaching of God out of the Scriptures.'

The Bishop of Ely was determined to get his revenge, so he suspended Latimer's preaching licence. This meant that he could not preach anywhere within the bishop's diocese, including Cambridge.

But we must never forget that Jesus said, 'I will build my church, and the gates of Hades will not overcome it' (Matthew 16:18). God is in control, and he provided a wonderful outlet for Latimer's continued preaching, in an area that was outside of the bishop's control, the Augustinian priory in Cambridge. The prior was Robert Barns and, hearing of the bishop's ban on Latimer, Barns invited him to preach in his pulpit on Christmas Eve.

LATIMER AND WOLSEY

Soon afterwards, Latimer's enemies brought his name before Cardinal Wolsey who hated the Reform movement and was merciless in dealing with so-called heretics. Latimer was summoned to appear before him to be questioned about his views of Martin Luther. Again, Latimer replied that he had not read him, he had read only the ancient Church fathers and medieval writers. Latimer referred to the incident with the Bishop of Ely, and what had subsequently occurred. Cardinal Wolsey was so impressed by Latimer that he granted to him his own personal licence permitting him to preach anywhere in England!

So, Latimer returned to Cambridge and launched himself into the preaching of the Gospel. His influence steadily growing, students flocked to hear him and many were converted. His practical sermons explained how the true and genuine Christian life should be lived.

An event then took place which made a deep impression on him and which he never forgot. His good friend Thomas Bilney was brought before Cardinal Wolsey and forced to recant. He was made to wander through the streets of London bareheaded with a bundle of sticks on his back. This signified that if he were to wander from the fold again, he would be burned at the stake. Bilney returned to Cambridge a broken man with his sense of guilt for having denied the true faith making him inconsolable.

Cardinal Wolsey died in 1530, whereupon Latimer's opponents seized the opportunity to attack his right to preach, but he remained adamant and he continued in his ministry. He came to the attention of King Henry VIII himself and was invited to preach before the court in March 1530. How would the King react to his preaching?

LATIMER AND KING HENRY VIII

Remarkably, King Henry VIII was delighted with Latimer and his preaching. He was made one of the King's chaplains and, along with several others, was appointed to draw up a list of the best religious books available in the land. Great compliment as this was,

Latimer found that court life was not for him. He had more in common with ordinary people than with court officials. Through some influential friends, he was appointed to a little country parish in the county of Wiltshire in the west of England. By January 1531, he found himself Rector of a small parish, no longer with any rich or influential people in his congregation, just simple and relatively uneducated people who found his preaching very beneficial.

Yet even here, his preaching could not go unnoticed; he was England's finest preacher at the time. The priests of the established church still considered him a heretic and feared the influence he was having on so many. A fellow reformer wrote of him, 'None except the stiff-necked and uncircumcised in heart went away without being affected with great hatred of sin and moved to godliness and virtue.' (Thomas Becon, *The Jewel of Joy*)

ACCUSED OF HERESY

At this time, other reformers were being persecuted, chiefly at the hands of two men, Bishop Stokeley of London and Sir Thomas More, the Chancellor of England. Such persecution was unconstitutional but, inconsistent and ambivalent man that he was, King Henry turned a blind eye. In Wiltshire, Latimer was outside Stokeley's jurisdiction, but in 1531 on a visit to London he was persuaded to preach. Much of the sermon was directed against the clergy in general and Stokeley in particular, but yet again Latimer escaped the bishop's clutches, on account of King Henry's high opinion of him personally. But Stokeley was not to be beaten. Through devious means he was able to summon Latimer to appear before him and in January 1532 Latimer stood accused of heresy. After several days, Latimer noticed that the furniture in the room had been moved around, the fire was out and a cloth had been draped over the fireplace. As he listened, he could hear the squeak of a pen recording every word he said whenever he was being questioned. One of the bishops actually asked him to speak up as he was rather deaf. Latimer knew full well that they were trying to trap him.

At first he answered all questions competently, but further issues were continually raised. As the case dragged on, he was ordered to recant or be excommunicated. At first he refused; he was excommunicated and awaited his fate. His life hung in the balance, as some sort of compromise was being discussed behind the scenes. What actually happened is unclear but it is widely thought that the King himself stepped in and asked Latimer to obey the bishops. Whatever the case, Latimer recanted. He had to apologise publicly to Stokeley and plead humbly for release from excommunication. This he did and was received back into the church. This has been described as the darkest page in Latimer's history.

In August of 1532, the Archbishop of Canterbury, William Wareham, died. At this time Henry was wanting to divorce his first wife, Catherine of Aragon, in order to marry Anne Boleyn. He wanted to appoint a successor to Wareham who would support Henry himself rather than the Pope. Thomas Cranmer, himself a supporter of reform, was appointed, which brought a new spiritual climate to the country, a ray of light after much darkness.

LATIMER MADE BISHOP

Cranmer set about looking for what could be called 'evangelical support' among the bishops. At this time there were several vacancies for bishops to be appointed. In August 1535, Latimer was made Bishop of Worcester. The whole cause of the Reformation was being strengthened but Latimer never saw himself as an administrator, he was first and foremost a preacher. He was often asked to preach at court where Anne, the new Queen, loved to hear him and even, it is said, accepted his private rebukes. However, before long Henry tired of Anne in favour of Jane Seymour, for which Latimer even dared to rebuke the King.

As bishop, he found some of his duties burdensome. When the monasteries came under review, he was appalled to find how far they had deviated from their vows of celibacy and poverty. Corruption and deception were everywhere. In 1536, many monasteries were closed down. Latimer took the opportunity to say in one of his sermons, 'Look at the man and woman living together piously in the fear of God, keeping his Word and active in the duties of their calling. They form a religious house, one that is truly acceptable to God. Pure religion consists, not in wearing a hood but in visiting the fatherless and the widows and in keeping oneself unspotted from the world. What has hitherto been called a religious life was an irreligious life, hypocrisy.'

Thus the Reformation cause in England was gaining strength, but Satan is ever active. In 1539 what was known as the 'whip of six strings' was given royal assent, and this again set the Reformation back. It consisted of six main articles: the real presence of Christ in the sacrament; the denial of the communion cup to ordinary people; the celibacy of the clergy; the obligation of monastic vows; the benefit of private masses and private confession to a priest.

This statute was in effect a re-establishment of former church teaching within the Church of England. Convinced this was wrong, both Cranmer and Latimer refused to accept these articles. The king, however, gave his assent on the 28 June 1539, and three days later Latimer resigned as bishop. Henry was incensed and ordered Latimer to be taken into custody in London, but for both political and personal reasons Henry allowed Cranmer to remain as Archbishop of Canterbury. Latimer was kept in seclusion and forbidden to preach for eight years. In Henry's last year, Latimer found himself in the Tower of London.

A NEW KING

King Henry VIII died in January 1547 and a new era dawned for the reformers. Henry was succeeded by the boy king, Edward VI, who, in spite of his youth, was a genuine supporter of the Reformation, and Hugh Latimer was immediately set free. He had used this period of imprisonment to establish further his biblical beliefs. By now he was in his sixties, but the next seven years were perhaps his most fruitful of all. He frequently preached to the young king yet he also reached the ordinary people. As one writer commented, 'No other reformer sowed the seeds of sound biblical teaching so widely and effectively among the lower classes of England as did Hugh Latimer.'

The reason for this was his grasp of the New Testament emphasis on preaching. He was very aware that it pleased God 'Through the foolishness of what was preached to save those who believe.' In one sermon he asks the question, 'Who is the most diligent bishop in all of England? Who surpasses all the others in doing his duty? I will tell you, it is the devil. He is the most diligent preacher of all. He is never away from his parish. You will never find him unoccupied. When the devil is present and has his plough working, then away with books and up with candles, away with Bibles and up with beads, away with the light of the Gospel, and up with the light of candles. There never was such a preacher in England as the devil is.'

For some reformers the role of baptism in bringing about true conversion was a source of confusion. While for Latimer, preaching was clearly the way that this happened as he often said, 'By the Word of the

living God, by the Word of God preached and opened
– that is how our new birth comes about.'

A NEW QUEEN

Sadly for the reformers, Edward VI died in July 1553
at the age of just sixteen. What might have happened
had he lived, we will never know. He was succeeded by
Mary Tudor, daughter of Henry VIII and Catherine
of Aragon, a zealous and extreme Catholic, who hated
the Reformation. She has gone down in history with
the title 'Bloody Mary' because before her reign of
terror came to an end, some 285 men and women
had died for the cause of the true Gospel.

Hugh Latimer was summoned to appear before the
Lord Chancellor. Friends encouraged him to make his
escape to the continent of Europe but, knowing the
effect that this would have on others, Latimer refused
to go. Yet he sensed what his fate would be. Along
with Cranmer, Bishop Nicholas Ridley, John Bradford
and Princess Elizabeth, Queen Mary's half-sister who
would later become Queen Elizabeth I, Latimer yet
again found himself in the Tower of London. In
January 1554 there was a political rebellion led by
Sir Thomas Wyatt which failed. Wyatt and a large
number of his followers were also thrown into the
Tower of London. The advantage of this to Latimer
and his friends was that they were all herded together
into the same cell so that they were able to enjoy
rich Christian fellowship together, reading the Bible,
praying and discussing Bible teaching.

After some months this came to an end, as news came that Cranmer, Ridley and Latimer were to be moved to Oxford. Bradford was in fact the first to be burnt to death, in London on 1 July 1555. Latimer, Cranmer and Ridley were sent to Oxford to face the most eminent theologians of the church. Inevitably, the matter of the Mass arose in the discussion. For anyone who did not accept the Mass, the only outcome was excommunication. All three men flatly denied the doctrine of transubstantiation and, as a result, were condemned to burn as heretics.

LATIMER'S DEATH AND LEGACY

In October 1555, Latimer and Ridley were taken from their cells to face the flames. They had been kept apart for weeks and so they greeted each other with joy. They were led past the prison where Cranmer was housed. He was brought out so that he might see them, but he was not permitted to speak to them. A large crowd had gathered to witness their execution. The regulation sermon which was preached to all heretics was delivered. Latimer and Ridley begged permission to reply to this sermon but they were refused. They accepted the decision and stood firm.

Nicholas Ridley said, 'Be of good heart brother, for God will either lessen the fury of the flames or else strengthen us to abide them.' And so, in Oxford, the two men were burnt to death, as many onlookers wept. It is known that at least one man was converted there and then. As they went to the stake, Latimer's words rang out, words which have gone down in history, words which were wonderfully prophetic under the hand of a sovereign God, 'Be of good comfort Master Ridley and play the man. We shall this day, by God's grace, light such a candle in England as I trust shall never be put out.' Latimer died swiftly, probably from suffocation, but Ridley suffered a slow death.

Five months later, in March 1556, Cranmer was burnt at the stake. Mary Tudor died in 1558 and was succeeded by Elizabeth, the daughter of Henry VIII by Anne Boleyn. Though by no means complete, when Queen Elizabeth began her long reign, the Reformation was at least secure. The Scriptures, with their teaching of the Gospel of salvation through faith alone in Christ alone, had come to a firm foothold in England at last.

How grateful we should be to men like Cranmer, Ridley and Latimer, men who were willing to stand against error, even to the point of giving their own lives in order that truth might prevail. What if they had not been willing to stand up for truth? What sort of country might England have been historically? Thank God that Hugh Latimer, by his preaching and example, in his life and death did indeed help to 'light such a candle in England as has never since been put out.'

CHAPTER 7

George Whitefield

EARLY LIFE

George Whitefield was born in England in 1714, the youngest of seven children. His father died when he was only two years old, so it fell to his mother to bring him up. The family ran one of the foremost inns in Gloucester and he had to take on his share of the chores. As a child Whitefield loved acting, mimicking some of the preachers he heard. Due to his family's financial troubles, his early education was patchy but in 1732 he began attending Oxford University, working his way through college. There he met Charles Wesley, an Anglican student who encouraged Whitefield toward devout Christianity. Whitefield joined the 'Holy Club' led by Charles' brother, John. The club was dedicated to prayer, fasting, and other spiritual exercises as well as to doing good to the poor and underprivileged. They were mockingly called Methodists because of their disciplined lifestyle. During these years in Oxford, Whitefield came under deep conviction of sin and by God's grace, was converted. In June 1736 he was ordained as a minister of the Church of England and preached his first sermon the following week in his home town of Gloucester. The church was packed, probably because many knew that this 'local lad' had a great gift of oratory. There followed a complaint to the bishop, that Whitefield had driven fifteen people mad as a result of his sermon!

So a great work of God, the eighteenth century evangelical awakening in England began under his preaching in 1736, at the age of twenty-two. This was the beginning of a work which was to set both England and America 'on fire' during the next thirty years or so, with repercussions which continue to this day.

HIS THEOLOGICAL POSITION
Whitefield was strongly reformed in his doctrinal position. He believed that salvation is all of God, that the elect were chosen in Christ before the foundation of the world, and that by nature we are all spiritually dead, needing the new birth before we

can even respond to the Gospel. Even saving faith is the gift of God. At first he was a little uncertain in this theology but study of Scripture during his first voyage to America helped him to come to a settled position on these important doctrines. He remained faithful to the whole counsel of God throughout his life, and read and reflected the writings of the Puritans. He had hoped to establish a college but this was prevented by his relatively early death.

Because he had fellowship with others who he considered had sometimes deviated from the purer Gospel, such as the Wesleys and the Moravians, some have accused him of sharing their errors. This, however, was never true and he remained faithful to the 'reformed' faith until the end of his life.

HIS EXEMPLARY LIFE

Whitefield was a truly spiritual man, like all of us, not without defect, and filled in the early days with misguided zeal, but always willing to learn and seek to walk in ever closer biblical obedience.

His single-mindedness

If we sought a fitting epitaph for Whitefield, it would surely be the words, 'Not I but Christ.' He always aimed at what would further the Gospel rather than his own ideas and schemes. He never sought favour and refused it, if he believed the cause of Christ would suffer. For example, in 1748 he voluntarily stepped down from the leadership of the Calvinistic

Methodists to prevent unnecessary rivalry between himself and the Wesleyan Methodists. From that time onwards, he shared gospel work with Wesleyan Calvinists, Dissenters, Anglicans and any who would have him to preach saying, 'Let my name be forgotten, let me be trodden under the feet of all men, if Jesus may thereby be glorified.'

Personal sanctification

This point is best illustrated by a letter written when returning to England in 1748, at the age of thirty-three:

> Alas! Alas! In how many things I have judged and acted wrong, I have been too rash and hasty…I have often used a style too apostolical…been too bitter in my zeal…I frequently wrote and spoke in my own spirit, when I thought I was writing and speaking with the assistance of the Spirit of God…I bless him for ripening my judgement a little more, for giving me to see … and correct some of my mistakes.

He subsequently revised his journals to reflect this change of attitude. His true humility is evidenced by a statement in reply to the question of whether he expected to see John Wesley in heaven, 'I fear not, he will be much nearer the throne than me.'

As a peacemaker

John Fletcher, one of Whitefield's assistants, spoke of him as 'the peacemaker'. This was seen in his handling of a difficult situation where the Wesley brothers had almost fallen out over John Wesley's plans for marriage.

Whitefield was able, to a large extent, to bring them together and prevent an open breach which would have divided the Methodist movement, or more likely 'scattered it to the winds'.

He was blamed for many things that were never true. Even his American friend, pastor Gilbert Tennent, became cool towards him, due to reports that he had joined the Moravians. In response, Whitefield sent Tennent a copy of his sermons, which he was about to publish, asking him to write a preface. On reading the sermons, Tennent realised he had been mistaken and the friendship was restored. George Whitefield was always seeking to be at peace with all God's true children.

Full of good works

Whitefield was generous, often giving beyond his own resources. For most of his life he was in debt because of the responsibility he had assumed for an orphanage he had set up in Georgia, America. He referred to it as 'a home for 100 but hearts for 10,000.'

A rather amusing incident illustrates his generosity. It occurred when on a visit to Scotland. Whitefield gave a significant sum of money for those days (five guineas) to help a widow, for which a friend with him reproved him. On their travels that day, they were held up by a highwayman who not only took all their money but made Whitefield exchange his coat for the highwayman's rather tattered one. Whitefield commented to his friend that the money was better helping the widow than in the highwayman's pocket. When they later examined the highwayman's jacket they found 100 guineas in one of the pockets!

He helped in every way he could, wherever there was a need. He paid for housing in London for the elderly and helped poor parents to pay for the education of their children. He even sent money to relieve distress after a fire in the American city of Boston had destroyed many houses.

HIS EXTENSIVE LABOURS

He preached 18,000 times in his thirty-four years as an evangelist, generally twice a day, and three times on Sundays. He made seven visits to America, involving thirteen crossings of the Atlantic Ocean by sailing ship, as well as fifteen visits to Scotland. He visited every county in England and Wales with the intention of returning to each one, following a similar pattern to the apostle Paul; Whitefield and Paul did indeed have much in common.

During one of his two visits to Ireland, he nearly met his death at the hands of a Catholic mob. He also had responsibility for two churches in London and carried on an extensive correspondence. Yet he repeatedly said, 'Oh that I could begin something for God!'

HIS INFLUENCE ON THE GREAT

The Countess of Huntingdon, a very well-known and wealthy lady at that time, was converted largely as the result of Whitefield's preaching and opened her home to invite other important people to hear the preaching of the Gospel. Some were converted. The Prince of Wales, the heir to the throne, was deeply affected by Whitefield's preaching, but died suddenly. The historian Dallimore comments on the effect of Whitefield's ministry among the great,

> The gatherings in Chelsea and North Audley Street, were profoundly interesting spectacles; and never till the day of judgement will it be ascertained to what extent the preaching of the youthful Whitefield affected the policy of some of England's greatest statesmen and moulded the character of some of its highest aristocratic families. (Arnold Dallimore, *George Whitefield*)

As a result of his visits to America, Whitefield became a lifelong and firm friend of Benjamin Franklin, one of the Founding Fathers of the United States, and Whitefield constantly sought to present the Gospel to him. Sadly, though impressed, Franklin was spiritually unaffected and remained a humanist.

His marriage

There are conflicting views about the happiness of Whitefield's marriage, but although there were many difficulties it was also a source of joy to him.

The circumstances of his meeting and marrying his wife, Elizabeth, are both amusing and sad. His friend Howell Harris had fallen in love with Elizabeth James, but did not want to marry. He wrote to Whitefield asking him to help with this difficult situation. Eventually, it was in fact Whitefield and Elizabeth who were married. Although resigned to the outcome, Harris was deeply grieved and took many years to get over it.

Soon after they were married, Elizabeth accompanied Whitefield on one of his trips to America, but travelling did not suit her and after that she preferred to stay at home. Whitefield built a house for her next to their chapel in London and she lived there most of the time. Only one live child was born to them, but he lived for only four months. Despite several miscarriages and at least one stillbirth, there were no more children.

It was always a burden to George that he had to leave Elizabeth so much to fulfil his preaching ministry, but it was something which she had accepted from the start of their marriage.

When she died he said, 'I feel the loss of my right hand daily.'

HIS DEATH

Many of the greatest servants of God were remarkable in their deaths and George Whitefield was no exception.

On Saturday 29 September 1770, he was in Exeter, New England. He sensed that the sermon he was preaching on that occasion would be his last. In his prayer before the sermon he said, 'Lord Jesus, I am weary in thy work, but not of thy work.' Towards the end of the sermon he also said, 'I go to a rest prepared ... My sun is about to set, no, it is to rise to the zenith of immortal glory.' Following the sermon he went to the home of his friend Jonathan Parsons in Newburyport, Massachusetts. After eating, he was about to go to bed early, but found a crowd gathered at the door, begging him to preach.

> Unwilling despite his weariness to forego any opportunity to declare the gospel, he responded to the request and stood on the landing, halfway up the stairs, candle in hand, preaching Christ. He was soon greatly alive to his subject and becoming heedless of time he continued to speak, till finally the candle flickered, burned itself out and died away. That dying flame and burned-out candle were representative that evening of the man himself and of his life. (Arnold Dallimore, *George Whitefield*)

He woke several times during the night, complaining about his asthma. At 4.15 a.m. he requested some warm gruel to help his asthma, which he said was 'choking him'. At five in the morning he went to the window, panting for breath, and said, 'I am dying.' The doctor was called, but nothing could be done for him. At 6 a.m. he died.

Should he die in America, he had previously requested to be buried beneath the pulpit of the church of his friend in Newburyport. His wish was granted and that is where his remains lie to this day.

In the opinion of many, George Whitefield was the greatest preacher England has ever known; he ranks without doubt among Reformers, Puritans and, one would almost say, Apostles in greatness.

Selected Biography

Arnold Dallimore, *George Whitefield* (Banner of Truth Trust, 1980

S.M. Houghton, *Sketches from church History* (Banner of Truth Trust, 1980)

Rev. J.A.Wylie, *The History of Protestantism, Volume 1*, (Cassel, Petter & Galpin, c.1880)

Serving **ST** *Today*

GRACE BAPTIST MISSION

About Serving Today

- In production since 2002 by the Radio Department of Grace Baptist Mission.

- A radio programme dedicated to supporting pastors and church leaders, mainly in developing countries.

- Over 700 programmes produced to date, *Serving Today* provides guides to preaching from various Bible books, help with pastoral issues, doctrine overviews, biblical perspectives on topical matters.

- Can be heard through TWR-Africa and other local stations across Africa, and via the internet (go to www.gbm.org.uk/radio)

- *'The Serving Today broadcasts are the only ones I know of that are specifically directed at pastors. It teaches pastors how to construct a sermon and also gives advice and guidance when dealing with a congregation.'* (as described by TWR-Africa)

- Also available to individual pastors and church leaders in the following ways:

on CD (MP3 format) together with a copy of the follow-up booklet sent by post as each series is completed. (This option is specifically for the support of those with limited access to resources.)

by weekly email as an MP3 attachment

To receive *Serving Today* in either of these ways, please contact us at the address below:

Serving Today
GBM Radio
12 Abbey Close
Abingdon
Oxfordshire OX14 3JD
(UK)

Email: radio@gbm.org.uk
Web: www.gbm.org.uk/radio

Follow us on Twitter:
@ServingTodayGBM

Please pray for the ministry of Serving Today.

CHRISTOPHER CATHERWOOD

FIVE LEADING
REFORMERS

Lives at a watershed of history

MARTIN LUTHER
THOMAS CRANMER
JOHN CALVIN
JOHN KNOX
ULRICH ZWINGLI

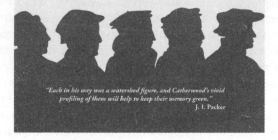

*"Each in his way was a watershed figure, and Catherwood's vivid
profiling of them will help to keep their memory green."*
J. I. Packer

ISBN 978-1-84550-553-0

Five Leading Reformers

Lives at a Watershed of History

CHRISTOPHER CATHERWOOD

Christopher Catherwood summarises the lives of Martin Luther, John Calvin, Ulrich Zwingli, Thomas Cranmer and John Knox. He unlocks the motivation, the power and drive that pushed these men to risk their position, their livelihoods and their lives.

Christopher Catherwood, a writer abreast of ongoing historical study of the period and aware of the spiritual issues hanging on the chain of events, tracks five major players from the cradle to the grave: Luther, Zwingli, Calvin, Cranmer, Knox. Each in his way was a watershed figure, and Catherwood's vivid profiling of them will help to keep their memory green.

J. I. PACKER,
Well known author & Board of Governors' Professor of Theology,
Regent College, Vancouver, Canada

Christopher Catherwood's fluent style brings out the broad sweep of a spiritual movement which transcended national barriers and has left a permanent mark on Europe and in the wider world. He shows how five men of very different personality and outlook could all be caught up in the same experience of a life transformed by the power of God. The portraits are painted "warts and all" but the message is clear - God can and does use the weak and imperfect things of this world to proclaim his message of salvation in Christ to all who believe.

GERALD BRAY,
Research Professor, Beeson Divinity School,
Samford University, Birmingham, Alabama

Christian Focus Publications

Our mission statement –

STAYING FAITHFUL
In dependence upon God we seek to impact the world through literature faithful to His infallible Word, the Bible. Our aim is to ensure that the Lord Jesus Christ is presented as the only hope to obtain forgiveness of sin, live a useful life and look forward to heaven with Him.

Books in our adult range are published in four imprints:

CHRISTIAN
FOCUS

Popular works including biographies, commentaries, basic doctrine and Christian living.

CHRISTIAN
HERITAGE

Books representing some of the best material from the rich heritage of the church.

MENTOR

Books written at a level suitable for Bible College and seminary students, pastors, and other serious readers. The imprint includes commentaries, doctrinal studies, examination of current issues and church history.

CF4•K

Children's books for quality Bible teaching and for all age groups: Sunday school curriculum, puzzle and activity books; personal and family devotional titles, biographies and inspirational stories – because you are never too young to know Jesus!

Christian Focus Publications Ltd,
Geanies House, Fearn, Ross-shire,
IV20 1TW, Scotland, United Kingdom.
www.christianfocus.com
blog.christianfocus.com